"*Dark Agents* is a classic tale with a contemporary edge. Through this work, Scarlet has given the world a gift by which to better identify, understand, and overcome our own monsters."

> —**Christine Boylan,** television writer and producer of *The Punisher*, *Once Upon a Time*, and *Cloak & Dagger*; and cofounder of Bespoke Plays

"In *Dark Agents*, through Janina Scarlet's skills and expertise in helping her patients cope with depression, anxiety, and post-traumatic stress disorder (PTSD), she has managed to craft a fun, adventurous, and compassionate story that is not only engaging, but quite educational, too."

> —**Deric A. Hughes**, writer and co-executive producer for *Arrow*, *Scream: Resurrection*, and *The Flash*

"Not since Yoda trained Luke has a story so accurately addressed the importance of a hero training not just their body, but their mind. Scarlet weaves real therapeutic practices seamlessly into her narrative so the reader can grow right alongside Violet and her friends."

> —**Lora Innes,** author and artist whose works include *The Dreamer* and *Wynonna Earp*

"Janina Scarlet entertains, educates, and enlightens with *Dark Agents*! Fun and fast-paced, this graphic novel will start a lot of important conversations! Brava!"

> —**Jonathan Maberry,** New York Times bestselling author of *Black Panther: Doomwar* and *V-WARS*

"It's a rare gift to have a great fantasy story that teaches valuable real-world lessons about coping with trauma. *Dark Agents* gives you all of that and more."

> —**Greg Weisman,** creator of *Gargoyles*, and writer and producer of *Young Justice*

"Maybe you feel broken by the things that have happened. But what if you knew that every single one of us, everyone, has a superpower? And, what if your superpower is there to be discovered in the midst of your deepest fears? Read *Dark Agents* and let the discovery begin."

—**Kelly G. Wilson, PhD,** author of *Mindfulness for Two*, and coauthor of *Acceptance and Commitment Therapy*

DARK AGENTS

BOOK ONE

Violet and the Trial of Trauma

JANINA SCARLET, PhD

Illustrations by
VINCE ALVENDIA

Instant Help Books
An Imprint of New Harbinger Publications, Inc.

Publisher's Note

This publication is designed to provide accurate and authoritative information in regard to the subject matter covered. It is sold with the understanding that the publisher is not engaged in rendering psychological, financial, legal, or other professional services. If expert assistance or counseling is needed, the services of a competent professional should be sought.

Printed in China

Distributed in Canada by Raincoast Books

Copyright © 2020 by Janina Scarlet and Vince Alvendia
Instant Help Books
An imprint of New Harbinger Publications, Inc.
5674 Shattuck Avenue
Oakland, CA 94609
www.newharbinger.com

Cover design by Amy Shoup

Illustrations by Vince Alvendia

Color by Wellington Alves

Lettering by Thomas Zahler

Acquired by Ryan Buresh

All Rights Reserved

Library of Congress Cataloging-in-Publication Data

on file

22   21   20
10   9   8   7   6   5   4   3   2   1

First Printing

DARK AGENTS

BOOK ONE

Violet and the Trial of Trauma

Long ago, brothers Zeus, Hades, and Poseidon agreed to split up the world into three realms — Land, Underworld, and Sea.

Hades, who pulled the shortest straw, inherited the Underworld.

Putting behind him his despair over his bleak inheritance, Hades sought to bring justice and the rule of law to all three realms. He created the Underworld Intelligence Agency (UIA), a group of magically gifted mortals and immortals, all highly trained in magical law enforcement.

These Dark Agents are pledged to keep order and peace among magical and nonmagical beings alike, and to shield mortals from the cruelest whims of the gods — and of other power-hungry beings...

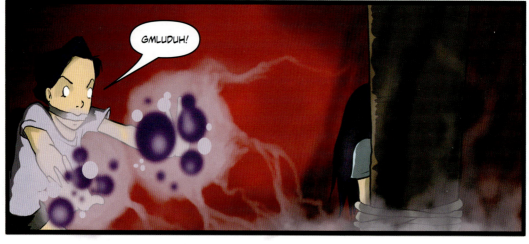

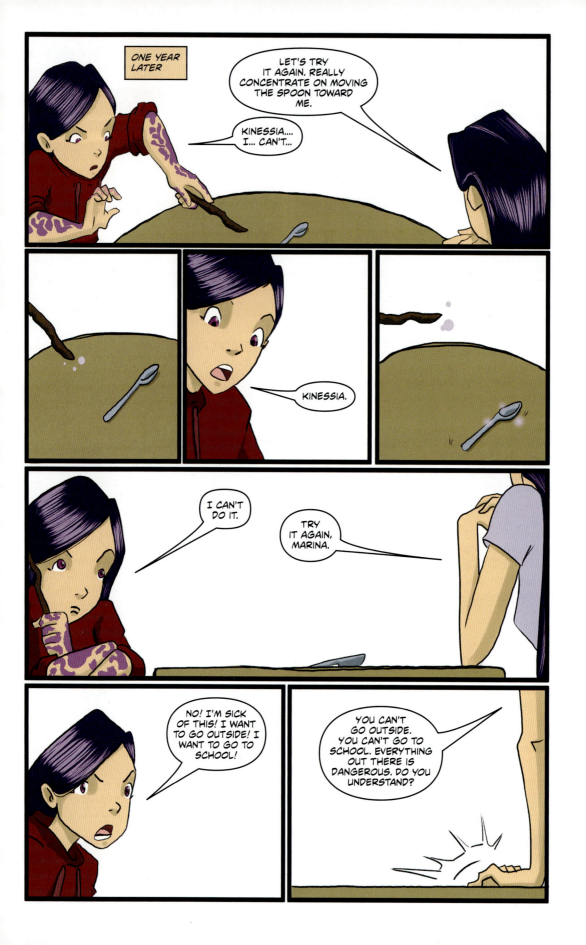

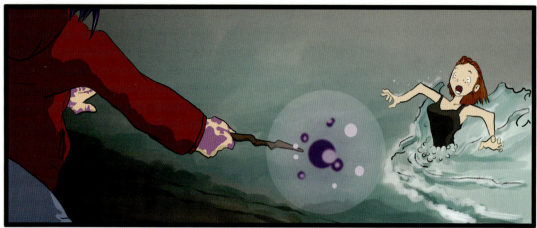

UNDERWORLD, THREE MONTHS LATER

THANKS.

CASSIE...

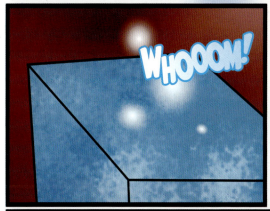

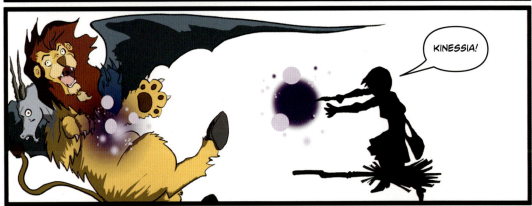

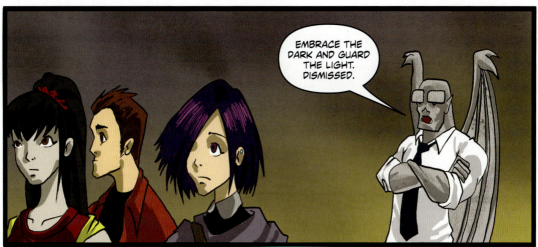

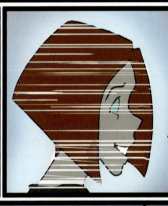

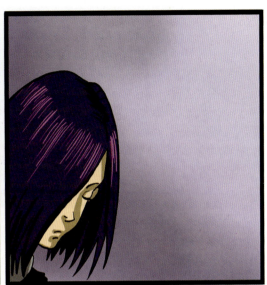

therefore these symptoms any Dark Agents experience or witness one or more traumatic events. Traumatic events, such as mortal near-death experiences, loss of loved ones, loss of ability, consistent threats or bullying can leave invisible scars. Although many recover from trauma naturally, others might develop posttraumatic stress disorder, or PTSD. You might have PTSD if you've experienced these symptoms for at least 1 month after the traumatic event:
1. Nightmares or flashbacks of the traumatic event
2. Increased anger
3. Being overly cautious, looking for danger everywhere
4. Difficulty trusting yourself or others
5. Avoidance of talking about the traumatic event or encountering reminders of the traumatic event

I DON'T HAVE IT.

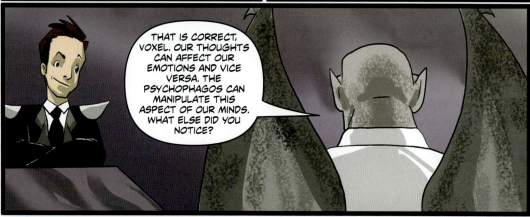

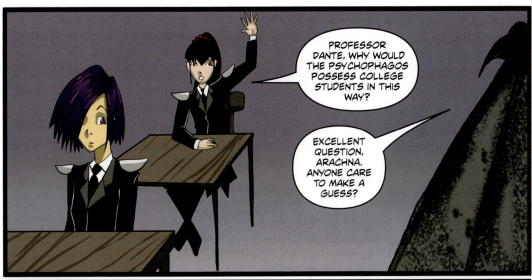

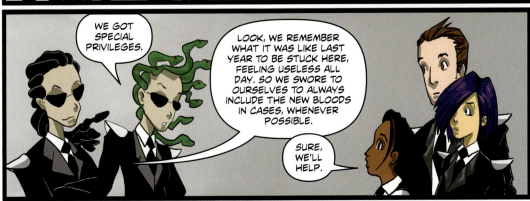

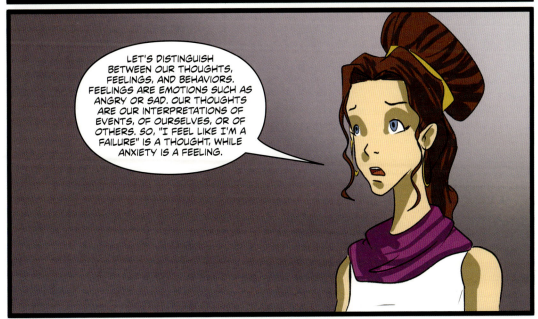

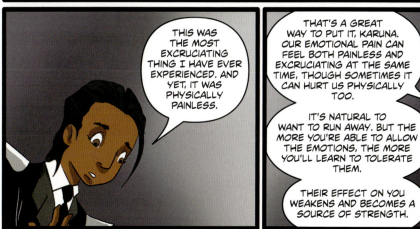

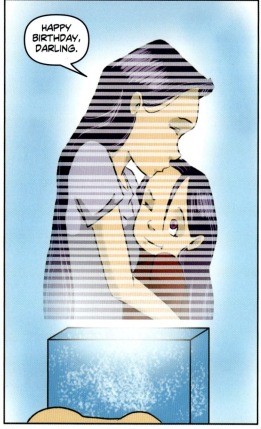

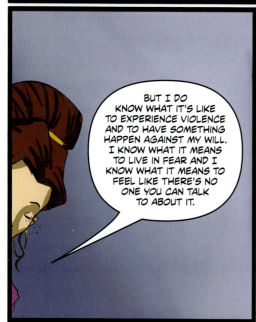

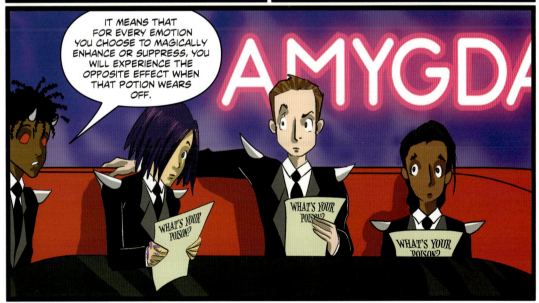

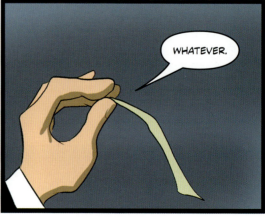

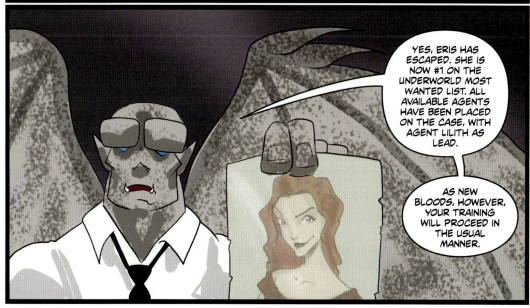

The Portal System

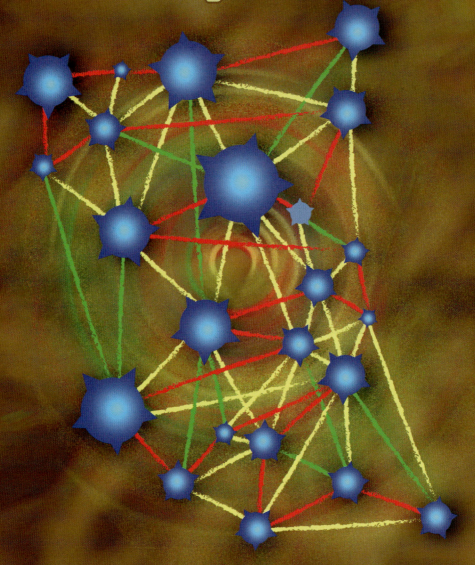

8

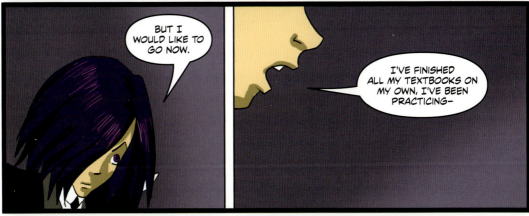
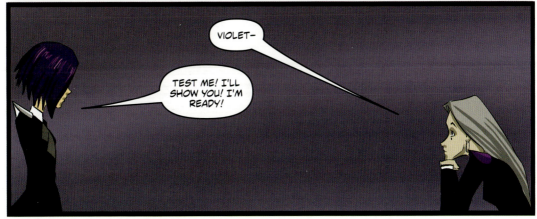

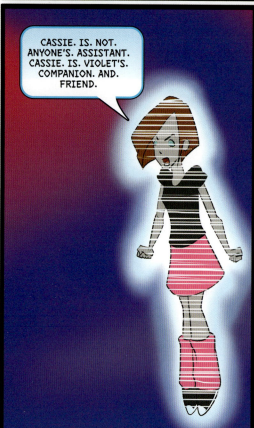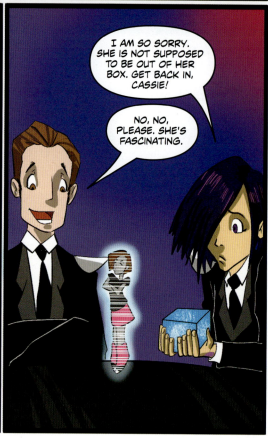

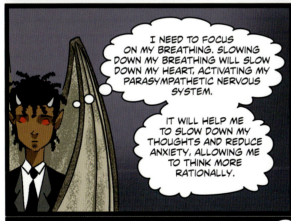

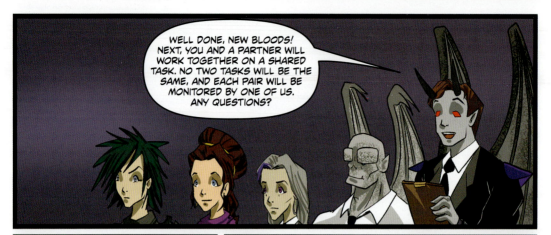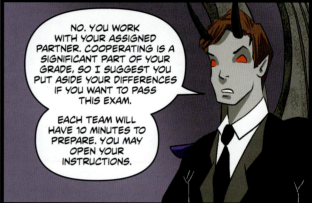

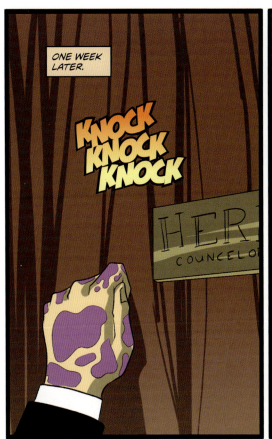

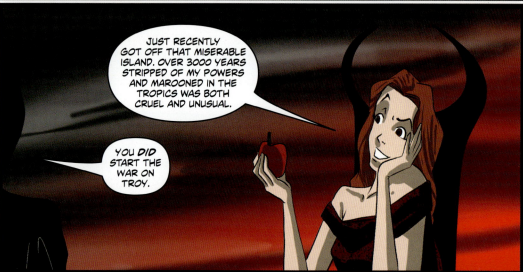

Janina Scarlet, PhD, is a licensed clinical psychologist, an award-winning author, and a full-time geek. A Ukrainian-born refugee, she survived Chernobyl radiation and persecution. Scarlet immigrated to the United States at the age of twelve with her family, and later, inspired by the X-Men, developed Superhero Therapy to help patients with anxiety, depression, and post-traumatic stress disorder (PTSD). She has been awarded the United Nations Association Eleanor Roosevelt Human Rights Award for her book, *Superhero Therapy*. Her other books include *Harry Potter Therapy*, *Therapy Quest*, and *Super-Women*.

Illustrator **Vince Alvendia** is a freelance artist/illustrator, native to San Diego, CA. His work has been featured in the official souvenir books for San Diego Comic-Con International; and also created one of three exclusive library card designs for the San Diego Public Library, in conjunction with the 2017 Comic-Con. Vince has contributed art to indie comic anthologies; and also continues to contribute to group art shows at various galleries, centered around pop culture and comic books. He loves carne asada burritos and Chinese food, and enjoys annoying his wife and fellow geek, Sabrina, and their spawn of "geeklings."

More Instant Help Books for Teens
An Imprint of New Harbinger Publications

SUPERHERO THERAPY
Mindfulness Skills to Help Teens
& Young Adults Deal with Anxiety,
Depression & Trauma
978-1684030330 / US $17.95

STUFF THAT SUCKS
A Teen's Guide to Accepting What
You Can't Change & Committing to
What You Can
978-1626258655 / US $14.95

PUT YOUR WORRIES HERE
A Creative Journal for Teens
with Anxiety
978-1684032143 / US $16.95

**THE ANGER WORKBOOK
FOR TEENS,
SECOND EDITION**
Activities to Help You Deal with
Anger & Frustration
978-1684032457 / US $17.95

**DON'T LET YOUR EMOTIONS
RUN YOUR LIFE FOR TEENS**
Dialectical Behavior Therapy Skills for
Helping You Manage Mood Swings,
Control Angry Outbursts & Get
Along with Others
978-1572248830 / US $16.95

**THINK CONFIDENT,
BE CONFIDENT FOR TEENS**
A Cognitive Therapy Guide to
Overcoming Self-Doubt & Creating
Unshakable Self-Esteem
978-1608821136 / US $17.95

newharbingerpublications
1-800-748-6273 / newharbinger.com

(VISA, MC, AMEX / prices subject to change without notice)

Follow Us

Don't miss out on new books in the subjects that interest you.
Sign up for our **Book Alerts** at **newharbinger.com/bookalerts**